W9-BLY-828

DERRICK ROSE

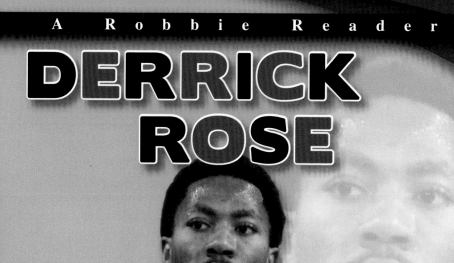

Marylou Morano
Kjelle

PUBLISHERS
P.O. Box 196
Hockessin, Delaware 19707
Visit us on the web: www.mitchelllane.com

Mitchell Lane
PUBLISHERS

Printing   1   2   3   4   5   6   7   8   9

A Robbie Reader Biography

Abigail Breslin
Adam Levine
Adrian Peterson
Albert Einstein
Albert Pujols
Aly and AJ
Andrew Luck
AnnaSophia Robb
Ariana Grande
Ashley Tisdale
Brenda Song
Brittany Murphy
Bruno Mars
Buster Posey
Charles Schulz
Chris Johnson
Cliff Lee
Dale Earnhardt Jr.
Darius Rucker
David Archuleta
Demi Lovato

Derrick Rose
Donovan McNabb
Drake Bell & Josh Peck
Dr. Seuss
Dwayne Johnson
Dwyane Wade
Dylan & Cole Sprouse
Emily Osment
Hilary Duff
Jamie Lynn Spears
Jennette McCurdy
Jesse McCartney
Jimmie Johnson
Joe Flacco
Jonas Brothers
Keke Palmer
Larry Fitzgerald
LeBron James
Mia Hamm
Miguel Cabrera

Miley Cyrus
Miranda Cosgrove
Philo Farnsworth
Raven-Symoné
Rixton
Robert Griffin III
Roy Halladay
Shaquille O'Neal
Story of Harley-Davidson
Sue Bird
Syd Hoff
Tiki Barber
Tim Howard
Tim Lincecum
Tom Brady
Tony Hawk
Troy Polamalu
Victor Cruz
Victoria Justice

Library of Congress Cataloging-in-Publication Data
Kjelle, Marylou Morano.
 Derrick Rose / by Marylou Morano Kjelle.
   pages cm. — (A Robbie Reader)
 Includes bibliographical references and index.
 Audience: Age: 5-9.
 Audience: Grade 1 to Grade 3.
 ISBN 978-1-68020-098-0 (library bound)
 1. Rose, Derrick—Juvenile literature. 2. Basketball players—United States—
Biography—Juvenile literature. I. Title.
 GV884.R619K54 2015
 796.323092—dc23
 [B]
                                                        2015003211
eBook ISBN: 978-1-68020-099-7

ABOUT THE AUTHOR: Marylou Morano Kjelle is a college English professor, free-lance writer, and photojournalist who lives and works in Central New Jersey. Kjelle has written dozens of books for young readers of all ages. She holds MS and MA degrees from Rutgers University, where she teaches freshman composition. When not teaching or writing, Marylou gardens, cooks, and bakes for her family and friends, watches movies, and she reads many books. She doesn't play basketball, but she enjoys watching games at the college where she teaches.

PUBLISHER'S NOTE: The following story has been thoroughly researched and to the best of our knowledge represents a true story. While every possible effort has been made to ensure accuracy, the publisher will not assume liability for damages caused by inaccuracies in the data, and makes no warranty on the accuracy of the information contained herein. This story has not been authorized or endorsed by Derrick Rose.

TABLE OF CONTENTS

Words in bold type can be found in the glossary.

Derrick puts his heart and soul into every game he plays. When he sets his sights on the basket, the opposing team had better watch out!

Most Valuable Player

When Derrick Rose plays basketball, he is a human tornado. At 6'3" (1.91 m) and 190 lbs. (86 kg), the **nimble point guard** for the Chicago Bulls blows past the opposing team's defense as he makes his way from one end of the court to the other. He flies to the basket, leaps and sends another ball swishing through the hoop.

Each year the National Basketball Association (NBA) honors one player as its best performer of the season. The award for Most Valuable Player (MVP) is the highest honor the **league** gives to an individual player. On May 4, 2011, the NBA named Derrick its MVP for the 2010-2011 basketball season.

Derrick received the award at the United Center, a sports **venue** in Chicago. That night the stands were filled with cheering fans who had come out to watch the Chicago Bulls play the Atlantic Hawks in the second game of the Eastern Conference playoffs. NBA **commissioner** David Stern presented Rose with the MVP award before the game.

"In a team of valuable players, you are most valuable," Stern said to Rose as he handed him the bronze MVP trophy.

Rose held the award high above his head for all to see. Yet, even in this moment of glory, Derrick did not forget his roots. "This here is for the city of Chicago more than anything else," he said. "I appreciate it, my family appreciate[s] it and my organization appreciate[s] it."

Derrick, who was 22 years old when he was named MVP, was the youngest player in NBA history to receive that award. It is an honor he still holds.

The MVP award given each year to an outstanding player is officially called the Maurice Podoloff Trophy. Maurice Podoloff was the president of the NBA from 1949-1963.

Whether playing for the USA team in the FIBA World Cup games or at home for the Chicago Bulls, Derrick is a powerhouse on the court.

"Mr. Basketball Player"

Derrick Martell Rose was born on October 4, 1988 in Chicago, Illinois. He grew up in Englewood, a neighborhood on Chicago's southwest side. Derrick's mother, Brenda is a stern but **affectionate** single parent. Derrick has three older brothers, Dwayne, Reggie, and Allan. When Derrick was a baby, his grandmother nicknamed him "Pooh" because she thought he **resembled** Winnie the Pooh.

It was tough growing up in Englewood where poverty, drugs, gangs, and guns ruled the streets. Derrick's life could have turned out badly in that environment, but his family protected him. Dwayne, Reggie, and Allan were more like father figures than brothers to Derrick. They saw that he got to school, to the gym, and to the basketball court and back safely. When Derrick did something wrong, he had to answer to his brothers.

"I didn't want to be in any trouble because I knew my mom or brothers would find out. I didn't want to hurt their feelings. I just tried to do everything right," Derrick said.

Dwayne, Reggie, and Allan kept Derrick out of trouble by teaching him how to play basketball. When he was in elementary school, Derrick and a few of the other boys in the neighborhood would shoot hoops in nearby Murray Park. Derrick loved playing basketball so much that he played from early morning till after dark, even though the court did not have lights. He even played when it was raining and snowing. Derrick was usually the youngest player on the court, and he quickly learned ways to outwit his heavier and taller opponents. He was good at running and passing, so point guard became his favorite position. It didn't

Derrick and his team members led Team USA to a gold medal in the 2010 FIBA World Championships.

Derrick has had his share of victories on the court, but he has also had his share of setbacks. After each injury, Derrick has worked hard to recover his health and strength.

take long for people to notice Derrick's talent on the court.

Derrick went to high school at Simeon Career Academy in Chicago where he played basketball for the Wolverines. In both his junior and senior years he led his team to state championships. That was the first time a Chicago public school had won back-to-back championships.

Derrick ended his high school career as a Wolverine with a 120-win/12-loss record and he was rated the nation's top high school point guard. *The Chicago Tribune* named Derrick "Illinois' Mr. Basketball Player" for 2007. People outside of Chicago were also starting to notice him. *USA Today* selected him as their national high school basketball player of the week.

It's easy to see why Derrick is called nimble. In a game between Memphis and UCLA, Derrick leaped between two opposing Tigers teammates and divided their defense.

Going Professional

As word of Derrick's basketball skills spread, many colleges tried to **recruit** him for their teams. Derrick chose the University of Memphis, and in 2007 he began playing point guard for the Memphis Tigers. Derrick led his team to a 38-win/ 2-loss record season, which placed the Tigers as the number one **seed** in the NCAA tournament. Memphis had to **forfeit** its thirty-eight wins, however, when it was rumored that Derrick did not take the **SAT** exam. Derrick was **disqualified** from the Tournament.

After one season of college basketball, Derrick announced he would enter the NBA **draft**. Derrick had grown up cheering for his hometown team, the Chicago Bulls. That year, the Bulls had the number one pick of players. On June 26, 2008, the Chicago Bulls announced that Derrick Rose would be the team's new point guard.

Derrick's first season (2008-2009) with the Chicago Bulls was an exciting one. He was just a **rookie**, but he was an **asset** to his team. He averaged close to seventeen points and six assists per game. He also made 47 percent of his shots. Statistics like these helped the Bulls

Derrick credits his mother, Brenda and brothers, Allan, Dwayne, and Reggie, for helping him become the player he is today. They insisted he stay out of trouble in his Englewood neighborhood and saw that he did.

advance to the NBA Eastern Conference play-offs. In his **debut** playoff game, Derrick scored 36 points. Only one other player in NBA history, Kareem Abdul-Jabbar, had scored as many points in a first playoff game.

On April 22, 2009, Derrick received the NBA's Rookie of the Year award. Many other honors followed. In the 2009-2010 season, he played in his first NBA All-Star game. In 2010, he and his team members led Team USA to a gold medal in the 2010 **FIBA** World Championship.

Derrick posed with his fellow USA team members during the 2014 FIBA World Basketball Championship in Bilbao, Spain, on August 31, 2014.

On Saturday, April 28, 2012, Derrick had to be helped off the court by his trainers late in the game against the Philadelphia 76ers. It was the first game of the Eastern Conference, and although Derrick had to leave the game, the Bulls won, 103-91.

CHAPTER FOUR

Injured

The 2010-2011 season was a record-breaking season for the Chicago Bulls. Their 62-win and 20-loss season was the best in NBA history. The following season, however, two events affected Rose's time on the court. The first was a strike between team owners and players over **revenues** and other issues. Although the season was shortened to 66 games, Derrick led the Chicago Bulls to the number-one seed in the Eastern Conference. Then, on April 28, 2012, during an NBA playoff game against the Philadelphia 76ers, Derrick tore a ligament in his left knee. He had **reconstructive** surgery and missed the rest of the playoffs as well as the rest of the 2012-2013 season.

To get healthy enough to play again Derrick first had to wear a brace to keep his knee **immobile**. He also had to perform months of physical therapy and special exercises. He was able to get back into the game for the 2013-2014 season. On November 22, 2013, ten games into the season, while playing the Portland Trail Blazers, he injured his right knee. Although that injury wasn't as bad as the one to his left knee, he still needed surgery and missed many games.

Derrick knows that getting injured is a risk every sports player takes. Over the years, he has sprained both ankles, hurt his toes, and injured his **hamstring** muscles. After every injury, his only focus has been to do what he needed to do to get back in the game.

"I'm back playing the sport I love. So for me, it feels like a new start," Derrick said after recovering from one of his knee injuries.

Derrick's number is 1. He chose that number when he became a Chicago Bull because he believes he plays more aggressively with that number on his uniform.

Derrick is a humble man who believes in helping others. He has used his skill as a basketball player to help those in need, both at home in Chicago as well as in other places, like Japan and Haiti.

Englewood Super Star

Derrick lives in Chicago and is the father of a son, Derrick Rose Jr., who was born on October 9, 2012. In spite of his talent and fame, he is a humble man who has never forgotten his Englewood roots. "[Englewood is] the reason I'm this person I am right now," Derrick said. Because he feels connected to that community, he returns to Englewood as often as he can. In 2011, he helped raise $15,000 to renovate the Murray Park basketball court where he played as a child. He even talks of re-doing the entire park, and maybe building a school and naming it after his mother.

Derrick's generosity goes beyond Englewood. In 2010, he helped Haitian earthquake victims by donating $1,000 for each point he scored in a game against the Phoenix Suns. When an earthquake struck Japan in March 2011, Rose donated $1,000 for each point he scored in a game against the Memphis Grizzlies. His donations have added up to thousands of dollars for those in need.

One of Derrick's personal goals is to lead the Chicago Bulls to an NBA

Derrick goes up for the shot against the Cleveland Cavaliers during Game Six of the NBA's Eastern Conference Semifinals at a home game at the United Center on May 14, 2015. The Cavaliers won 94-73.

Championship. Although basketball is an important part of Derrick's life, he doesn't want to only be known for sports. "[I] want to do everything right and be the best role model [I] could possibly be," Derrick said.

One thing is certain. Whether on the basketball court or off, the future looks bright for the Englewood All-Star Derrick Rose.

When he sets his sights on sinking a ball into the net, Derrick is unstoppable, as this Cleveland Cavaliers player learned during Game 2 of the Eastern Conference Semifinals on May 6, 2015. Derrick scored 14 points for the Bulls, but the Cavaliers took the game 106-94.

CHRONOLOGY

1988   Derrick Martell Rose is born on October 4.

2005   As point guard for Simeon Career Academy, Rose helps the Wolverines win the state championship.

2007   Rose leads the Wolverines to their second championship. The Chicago Tribune gives him the name "Illinois' Mr. Basketball Player." He enters the University of Memphis. He plays for the USA in the Nike Hoops Summit Game, and he plays in the McDonald's All-American game.

2008   Rose is the number-one pick of the NBA draft and he is chosen by the Chicago Bulls on June 26.

2009   Rose receives the "Rookie of the Year" award on April 22.

2010   Rose and his team members lead Team USA to a gold medal in the 2010 FIBA World Championship.

2011   Rose receives the NBA's "Most Valuable Player" award on May 4.

2012   Rose tears a ligament in his left knee on April 21 and he cannot play for the rest of the 2012-2013 season.

2013   Rose injures his right knee on November 22 and he cannot play for the rest of the 2013-2014 season.

2014   Rose returns to the court for the 2014–2015 season.

2015   After spending two seasons on the sidelines, Rose helps the Chicago Bulls make it to the Eastern Conference Semifinals.

STATISTICS

Year	Team	G	3PM-A	FTM-A	REB	AST	STL	BLK	TO	PTS
08-09	CHI	81	16-72	197-250	317	512	66	18	202	1,361
09-10	CHI	78	16-60	259-338	293	469	57	27	217	1,619
10-11	CHI	81	128-385	476-555	330	623	85	51	278	2,026
11-12	CHI	39	54-173	194-239	131	307	35	28	119	852
13-14	CHI	10	16-47	27-32	32	43	5	1	34	159
14-15	CHI	28	36-142	85-106	84	136	18	8	91	475
Career		313	268-879	1,238-1,520	1,187	2,090	266	133	941	6,492
All-Star		3	2-3	1-2	4	12	4	0	4	33

Legend

G- Games Played
3PM-A- 3 Points Made-Attempted
FTM-A- Free Throws Made-Attempted
REB- Rebounds
AST- Assists
STL- Steals
BLK- Blocks
TO- Turnovers
PTS- Points

Awards

2007 Illinois' Mr. Basketball
McDonald's All-American
USA Today All-USA First Team
Parade All-America First Team
EA Sports All-American First Team
All State Illinois

2008 NCAA Tournament All-Final Four Team
NCAA Tournament South Region MVP
NABC Third Team All-American

2009 NBA Rookie of the Year
NBA All-Rookie First Team
NBA Skills Challenge Champion

2010 NBA All-Star

2011 NBA Most Valuable Player
NBA All-Star
All-NBA First Team

2012 NBA All-Star

FIND OUT MORE

Books

Birle, Pete. *Chicago Bulls*. La Jolla, CA: Scobre Press, 2013.

Fishman, Jon M. *Derrick Rose*. Minneapolis: Lerner Publishing Group, 2014.

Hobin, Paul. *Derrick Rose: NBA's Youngest MVP*. Fort Wayne, IN: Sportszone, 2012.

Kelly, K.C. *Basketball Superstars*. New York: Scholastic, 2014.

Sandler, Michael. *Derrick Rose*. New York: Bearport Publishing, 2010.

On the Internet
The Chicago Bulls
    http://www.chicagobulls.com
Derrick Rose Official Website
    http://www.drosehoops.com
National Basketball Association
    http://www.nba.com

Works Consulted
"2007-08 Memphis Tigers Roster and Stats." *Sports Reference/College Basketball*. http://www.sports-reference. com/cbb/schools/memphis/2008/html

Aschburner, Steve. "Rose's roots: Family, coaches shaped MVP front-runner." *NBA Media Ventures.* April 6, 2011. www.nba.com/2011/news/features/steve_ aschburner/0406/rose-roots

Chicago Tribune Staff. "Derrick Rose: The Injury, Recovery, and Return of a Chicago Bulls Superstar." Agate Digital. 2013.

"Derrick Rose Receives the MVP Trophy." *YouTube.* www.youtube.com/watch?v=UyMEZ4TQ4b4

"Derrick Rose." *University of Memphis Athletics.* www.gotigersgo.com/sports/m-baskbl/mtt rose_ derrick00.html

"Derrick Rose Japan Donation: Giving $1,000 For Every Point Scored Friday To Earthquake And Tsunami Relief." *Huffington Post.* March 25, 2011. http://www. huffingtonpost.com/2011/03/25/derrick-rose-japan-donati_n_840603.htm

Dwyer, Kelly. Ball Don't Lie. "Derrick Rose tears the medial meniscus in his right knee, will need surgery, is out indefinitely." *Yahoo Sports.* November 23, 2013. http://sports.yahoo.com/blogs/nba-ball-dont-lie/derrick-rose-tears-medial-meniscus-knee-surgery-indefinitely-225500488-nba.html

FIND OUT MORE

Greenberg, John. "Derrick Rose is NBA MVP." *ESPN*. May 3, 2011. http://sports.espn.go/com/chicago/nba/news/story?id=6468133&campaign=rss&source=twitter&ex_cid=Twitter_espn_6468133

Jensen, Sean. "Derrick Rose keeps tough Englewood area close to his heart." August 27, 2011. Posttrib.chicagotribune.com/photos/galleries/index/htm?stories=5365750

"MVP Derrick Rose Honors His Mother." *CBS Chicago*. May 4, 2011. http://Chicago.cbslocal.com/2011/05/04/mvp-derrick-rose-honors-his-mother/

"NBA'S Youngest MVP Winners." *Sports Illustrated*. http://www.si.com/nba/photos/2014/05/06/youngest-nbamvp

Powers, Scott. "Bulls' Derrick Rose tears ACL." April 29, 2012. *ESPN*. http://espn.go.com/chicago/nba/story/-/id/7866701/2012-nba-playoffs-chicago-bulls-derrick-rose-suffers-torn-acl-philadelphia-76ers

"Rose named NBA's top rookie." *ESPN*. April 22, 2009. http://sports.espn.go.com/nba/news/story?id=4088433

Strotman, Mark. "Rose adds another chapter to 'new start' in win over Bucks." October 21, 2013. http://www.csnchicago.com/bulls/rose-adds-another-chapter-new-start-win-over-bucks

"Timeline," DRose—*The Official Website of Derrick Rose*. www.drosehoops.com

Velazquez, Francisco E. "Derrick Rose's Big Night Leads Pack Of Ten To Big Haiti Donation."*The Bleacher Report*, January 23, 2010. http://bleacherreport.com/articles/331289-roses-big-night-leads-pack-of-ten-to-big-haiti-donation

GLOSSARY

affectionate (uh-FECK-she-nit)—loving

asset (AS-et)—a desirable quality

commissioner (ka-MISH-e-ner)—a person who is in charge

debut (dey-BYOO)—a first public appearance

disqualified (dis-QWAL-i-fiid)—declared not eligible (proper or worthy) for the game or task

draft—selecting people for members or service or an athletic team

FIBA—the International Basketball Federation, founded in 1932

forfeit (FOR-fit)—to give up or lose

hamstring (HAM-string)—a tendon (connecting tissue between muscle and bone) at the back of the knee

immobile (ih-MO-bul)—not able to move or to be moved

league (leeg)—a group of athletic teams

nimble (NIM-bel)—quick and light in movement

point guard—the player who passes the ball to a player who can shoot

reconstructive (REE-kun-STRUK-tiv)—remaking or rebuilding something

recruit (ree-KROOT)—a new member of an organization

resemble (ree-ZEM-bul)—to look like something or someone

revenue (REV-en-yoo)—money or income raised from taxes or other sources

rookie (ROOK-ee)—an athlete playing a first season

SAT—Scholastic Aptitude Test, a test that colleges use to determine the admittance of students

seed—a position in a playoff or tournament

venue (VEN-yoo)—a place where an event is held

INDEX